YOUR PET HAMSTER

REVISED EDITION

A TRUE BOOK®

by

Elaine Landau

Children's Press®
A Division of Scholastic Inc.

New York Toronto London Auckland Sydney
Mexico City New Delhi Hong Kong
Danbury, Connecticut

Two sleeping golden hamsters

Content Consultant
Robin Downing, DVM, CVA, DAAPM
Hospital Director, Windsor Veterinary Clinic Windsor, Colorado

Reading Consultant
Cecilia Minden-Cupp, PhD
Former Director, Language and Literacy Program Harvard Graduate School of Education

Author's Dedication
Jeannie and Stephen Schwartz

The photograph on the cover shows a golden hamster. The photograph on the title page shows a golden hamster climbing out of a cup.

Library of Congress Cataloging-in-Publication Data
Landau, Elaine.
    Your pet hamster / by Elaine Landau.— Rev. ed.
        p. cm. — (A true book)
    Includes index.
    ISBN-10: 0-531-16798-4 (lib. bdg.)   0-531-15467-X (pbk.)
    ISBN-13: 978-0-531-16798-4 (lib. bdg.)   978-0-531-15467-0 (pbk.)
    1. Hamsters as pets—Juvenile literature. I. Title. II. Series.
SF459.H3L35 2006
636.935'6—dc22

                                                        2006004420

Contents

A hamster is small enough to hold in your hands.

How About a Hamster?

Are you looking for a cute, furry pet? Would you like one that is small enough to fit in the palm of your hand? Do you need a pet that doesn't take a lot of work? If that's the case, how about getting a hamster?

There are many great reasons for having a pet hamster. They won't take up much space in your home. They also don't cost much money to care for.

Hamsters store dry food in their cages. That means your family can safely leave your hamster at home for a couple of days at a time.

Best of all, hamsters are fun. People like watching them run on their wheels and climb their ladders. Tame hamsters even enjoy being held. Who could ask for more? A hamster may be just the pet for you.

A hamster climbs a little ladder in its cage.

Hamsters play in their glass cage at a pet store.

Selecting a Hamster

When you go to the pet store, all the hamsters seem cute. But how do you know which one to choose?

You should have a large selection of healthy hamsters. A young hamster should weigh at least 1½ ounces (43 grams).

Hamsters can be gold or white. They could have brown or beige spots. Different types, or **breeds**, of hamsters come in other colors. They can also be long-haired or have short hair.

The Chinese hamster is one type, or breed, of hamster.

This three-week-old hamster is too young to leave its mother.

Ask about the hamster's age before you buy it. It is best to pick a hamster that is about five weeks old. At this age, it is ready to leave its mother.

Don't buy a hamster that is more than a few months old. Hamsters only live for about two to three years, and you will want to have your pet for as long you can.

Hamsters usually do well with people. They like a lot of attention. But be careful not to rush things with your new little pet. Let your hamster get to know you and your scent before you try to pick it up.

A pet golden hamster and her two babies

The Most Common Hamster

The most common pet hamster is the golden or Syrian hamster. It is likely, however, that this animal has died out, or is **extinct**, in the wild.

In the past, these hamsters lived in the hot deserts of the Middle East. They escaped the heat during the day by staying in tunnels or holes in the ground called **burrows**. After the sun went down, they came out to search for seeds and insects to eat.

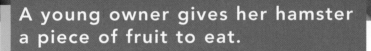

A young owner gives her hamster a piece of fruit to eat.

You might try feeding your hamster a treat from your hand. Let its body rest comfortably in your hands. A hamster has to know that you are not going to hurt it.

There are some other rules about handling hamsters. Never tease or poke a hamster. Don't lift a hamster by its tail, feet, or neck. Never pick up a sleeping hamster or blow on a hamster to wake it.

Don't expect a frightened animal to have a sense of humor. Hamsters have teeth and will nip you if they are alarmed. Hamsters are small living creatures. You must treat them gently and with care.

Taking Home a Healthy Hamster

A healthy hamster should have:

◀ a plump body and rounded head

◀ soft, silky fur

clear, bright eyes ▶

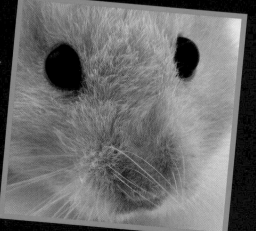

a slightly moist nose

 an active, alert nature

Pass up a hamster with:

* any bald spots on its fur
* watery eyes
* a runny nose
* small spots on its ears, nose, or stomach
* any type of injury, scabs, or scratches

A hamster explores its large cage.

Hamster Housing and Food

Every hamster needs its own cage or home. Even though a hamster is small, the cage should be big. These curious little animals need room to explore and play. A hamster's cage is its playground. Putting a hamster in a small cage is like taking away its recess time.

Pet stores offer different choices. There are plain, metal cages, or you can choose a plastic cage with long con-necting tubes. This kind of cage is like an underground burrow for your hamster.

Keep your hamster's cage clean. Scrub the cage once a week and rinse it out thoroughly. The cage should be dry before you put the hamster back in it.

Children watch a hamster play in its plastic cage.

Each week, spread a layer of 1 to 2 inches (2.5 to 5 centimeters) of fresh **wood shavings** on the bottom of the cage. Wood shavings are small strips of wood used for hamster bedding. You can buy bags of wood shavings at pet stores.

A hamster usually uses a corner of the cage as a toilet. Remove the soiled shavings from that area every two or three days.

You should replace your hamster's soiled bedding every few days.

Your hamster needs a healthy diet to stay active. A dry hamster food mixture of nuts, grains, and seeds is the best basic food. You can also buy crunchy treats to keep your hamster's teeth in good shape.

A hamster feeds on a nut.

Hamsters like to eat bits of fruit such as sliced apples.

Hamsters need fresh foods, too. Small amounts of fruits and vegetables add variety and a little water to your pet's menu. Most hamsters like carrots, corn, spinach, and apples.

Hamsters are **hoarders**. That means they like to store things. They fill their cheek pouches with food and then hide the food in their cages for later.

While you will want to keep your pet's cage clean, do not remove the stored food. That might upset the hamster. Don't feed your hamster too much of any fresh food. Those foods will spoil after a few days. Never feed your

This hamster's cheek pouches are full of food.

hamster candy or chocolate
because it can get stuck in
the hamster's cheek pouches.

A hamster drinks from a water bottle with a stainless steel spout.

Hamsters get most of the water they need from the food they eat. But they still need fresh water to drink every day.

A water bowl in a hamster cage will quickly become dirty. So buy a water bottle made for hamsters and rats. These bottles have a drinking tube to deliver clean water. The tube's spout is stainless steel, which your hamster can't gnaw.

Do your best to keep your hamster healthy.

Keeping Your Hamster Healthy

Hamsters are small, strong animals. With a proper diet and a clean home, they are likely to stay healthy. You can help by putting the cage in a place that isn't too hot or too cold for the hamster.

Hamsters are active mostly at night. They need to rest during the day. Do not wake your hamster if it is trying to sleep. Hamsters need a lot of rest to live a long life.

Hamsters sleep a lot during the day and play at night.

This hamster is grooming, or cleaning, its face.

Don't give your hamster a bath. Hamsters have natural oils that keep their fur soft and clean. They spend a lot of time **grooming**, or cleaning, themselves.

Hamsters can get illnesses that people have, such as the common cold. Do not pick up your hamster or get too close to it when you are sick. Ask friends and family members with colds to keep away from the hamster, too. It is always a good idea to wash your hands before and after handling your pet.

If your hamster becomes ill, take it immediately to a **veterinarian**, a doctor who

Check to make sure that your hamster is healthy.

treats animals. A veterinarian can give your hamster the care it needs.

A playful hamster pokes its head out of a cardboard tube.

Your Playful Hamster

A hamster is naturally playful.
You can help keep it that way.
Give your pet some interesting
toys, along with a spacious
cage.

Hamsters are natural
climbers. If its cage has bars
that go across, a hamster will

climb up on them. You can also buy small hamster ladders at pet stores.

However, hamsters love exercise wheels the most. Some hamsters run for 4 to 8 miles (6 to 13 kilometers) a night on these wheels!

Pet stores carry a lot of other hamster toys. Simple household items such as cardboard egg cartons or toilet paper rolls also make great playthings.

With an exercise wheel, a hamster can run for miles without leaving its cage.

Just make certain you pick toys made of materials that aren't dangerous to the hamster. The toys should not have sharp edges either.

Some owners only take their hamsters out of the cage to pet them. Other owners take their hamsters out often to run freely in the room.

If you let your hamster out, keep it in one room and close all the windows, doors, and

air vents. Be sure no other
family pets are in the room.

A roaming hamster peeks
out of a drawer.

A playful hamster can make a wonderful pet.

Stay in the room at all
times while your hamster is
on the loose and watch where

it goes. Hamsters are very small animals and can quickly slip out of sight. Don't take your eyes off your fast-moving pet! You must be sure to keep your hamster safe while it is out of its cage.

Watching a healthy hamster at play is like going to an animal show. Give your hamster the care and attention it needs, and your playful pet will delight you and your family.

To Find Out More

Here are some additional resources to help you learn more about hamsters:

 **Books**

Blackledge, Annabel. **Small Pet Care: How to Look After Your Rabbit, Guinea Pig, or Hamster**. DK Publishing, 2005.

Engfer, LeeAnne. **My Pet Hamster and Gerbils**. Lerner, 1997.

Fox, Sue. **Dwarf Hamster Care**. TFH Publications, 2003.

Ganeri, Anita. **Hamsters**. Heinemann, 2003.

Jeffrey, Laura S. **Hamsters, Gerbils, Guinea Pigs, Rabbits, Ferrets, Mice, and Rats: How to Choose and Care for a Small Mammal**. Enslow, 2004.

Petty, Kate. **Hamster**. Stargazer Books, 2005.

Silverstein, Alvin, Virginia Silverstein, and Laura Silverstein Nunn. **Pocket Pets**. Twenty-First Century Books, 2000.

Organizations and Online Sites

American Society for the Prevention of Cruelty to Animals (ASPCA)
424 East 92nd Street
New York, NY 10128
212–876–7700
http://www.aspca.org

This organization's site has extensive information on small pet care, including a brochure on hamster care that you can download.

The Hamster Site
http://www.thehamstersite. com/

This site has general hamster information and pictures, details about different types of hamsters, and some personal stories about rescued hamsters.

Hamsterific.com
http://www.hamsterific.com/

This site offers information on types of hamsters, hamster care, diet and nutrition, and other topics of interest to hamster owners, including a hamster glossary.

National Hamster Council
c/o National Secretary
PO Box 4
Llandovery, SA20 0ZH
United Kingdom
http://www.hamsters-uk.org/

The oldest hamster club in the world provides information on hamster care and the different hamster breeds as well as several hamster-related articles and stories.

Important Words

breeds specific types of animal

burrows animal tunnels or holes in the ground

extinct having died out

grooming cleaning

hoarders those who store things for later use

veterinarian a doctor who treats animals

wood shavings small strips of wood used for hamster bedding

Index

Meet the Author

Award-winning author Elaine Landau worked as a newspaper reporter, an editor, and a youth-services librarian before becoming a full-time writer. She has written more than 250 nonfiction books for young people, including True Books on dinosaurs, animals, countries, and food. Ms. Landau has a bachelor's degree in English and journalism from New York University as well as a master's degree in library and information science. She lives with her husband and son in Miami, Florida.